CW01511584

First Published in Great Britain in 2018

Text copyright © Nathan Burden, 2018

Printed by Amazon

The Art of Bad Management

How to Lose Staff and Demotivate People

Introduction

If you want to be the kind of manager who can't seem to keep a stable team of motivated, hardworking and dedicated people around you, then this book is for you! It will provide you with many ways in which to demotivate staff, to the point where they feel they must leave. This will ensure that you will never again have the stability and joy of a team which will perform to their best. Oh no. These ideas will make certain that you are always recruiting, repeating training and pulling your hair out about why the new team member (who only joined last week) doesn't know what they are doing.

Author's Warning

If, and I know it is unlikely, you want to lead a team of people who know they are valued and appreciated, willing to take risks, but ultimately deliver for you, then DON'T DO THESE THINGS. This will only lead to enjoyment of your job, satisfaction that you are allowing your underlings to develop their full potential and establish an excellent atmosphere in which to work. It will also lead to happy staff – and I'm sure you will agree, this must be avoided at all costs!

I mean, who wants happy, motivated, productive and creative staff...

1) Ask your team for ideas – then tell them the ideas are rubbish

One of the most effective strategies that the bad manager can employ is to lead meetings in which ideas are asked for, and then to systematically and ruthlessly rubbish any ideas that are put forward. This is particularly effective when the rest of the team all agree that it is a good idea, as you get to dig at more than one team member. If you want to be especially awful, you can even admit later to some members of the team that the idea was actually quite good, but you must make sure never to admit to this in public. Sowing discord amongst your team is an exceptional skill – give yourself bonus points!

How to set up the perfect scenario? First, make sure that all team members present believe that you don't have any ideas at all (even though you know what you want and are going to do it that way anyway). Second, make some kind of (apparently) sincere speech that you welcome all ideas, and that you value your team. You can now sit back and anticipate the moment when you can launch your attack!

Helpful hints

* Let a few suggestions go unpunished to start – it's like an ambush, but better!

* Don't let people finish their explanations – this will only allow the merits of the ideas to be stated and must be avoided at all costs.

* Glare at them, while they are talking, with an evil expression – practise this in a mirror at home, or on people in the supermarket!

* Make disparaging noises and grunts of exasperation – the louder the better.

* Make sure you mention all the reasons why the idea is bad – make up reasons if you can't think of any as these are the most dangerous ideas (you know, the ones that are actually really good and might make things better for everyone).

2) Ask experts to come and visit your team – then argue with them and tell them you disagree.

Every aspiring manager should remember one thing; they know best. Always. Even when confronted with experts who have proven expertise in their fields. I mean, why would an expert have anything valuable to say? Sure, they may have years of experience in a variety of settings and situations, some even come with professional qualifications, but let's face it – they don't know how the world really works do they? So, in order to combat this threat of competence and understanding contaminating your team, you should endeavour to argue with your guest expert at every available opportunity. And don't hold back either, make it loud, and public.

There may be times when you feel like you want to confuse your staff. The Ideal time is after a visit from an expert. First, apparently agree to some of what they advise. Later on, moan at your staff for doing things the new way! It's great to see the confusion on their faces as you catch them doing things as the expert suggested, only for you to be able to point out how wrong they are! The truly gifted 'Bad Manager' will have several experts visit each year and then mix and match different points from each, thus helplessly confusing their team.

Helpful hints

* Give the experts a really warm welcome so that they think you want to listen to them.

* When you argue – make sure you don't have suggestions yourself, just focus on the negatives.

* Why not try talking loudly to the person next to you about why you disagree with them while they are still talking to your team.

* If you call the meeting a training sessions, then staff will leave not knowing who to listen to, you or the expert – what a perfect situation.

3) Change the way you do something before giving it time to see if it works – repeat multiple times a year

Confusion. Disarray. Mayhem. Chaos. What a lovely set of words that could describe the way that your team feel. When staff know exactly what they are doing, and work as a cohesive unit, then terrible things like increased productivity happen. To avoid this, make sure that you never let that settled feeling descend upon the team. Nothing gets people worked up faster than telling them that they need to change how they are doing something again, and again, and again. Honestly, it really is a delight to see the life drain from their eager little faces when you announce that what you told them two weeks ago is now not right, and that they need to start doing it a different way.

Now the key here is to make sure that you don't ever give something enough time to understand if it works or not. If something doesn't produce the desired results instantly, then it obviously isn't working. Perhaps you could arrange for other senior leaders to also introduce changes at the same time, but then when they have been communicated, disagree with them and start to moan at your staff. For added impact, you could constantly question your team why things aren't being done like they were before the changes that you implemented and take pleasure in their feeble attempts to explain that they were 'told' to do it a different way. This technique works well when partnered with the 'arguing with the expert strategy' as your team will end up hopelessly confused.

Helpful hints

* Never have a clear understanding of how you want something done.

* Don't let more than a few weeks pass before changing something.

* Make sure you loudly criticise your own previously communicated ideas.

* Make sure your staff have no idea of how you expect something to be done.

4) Treat your staff as a number, not a person

Your staff are human, probably, which means that they have these annoying things called emotions and feelings. These dangerous little things can really bring people together in a shared understanding of life and so must be stamped out ruthlessly. The best way to do this is to treat your staff as if they are a robot off of a production line. Make sure they know that you just don't care about them, but see them just as a 'worker'. When applied correctly, this technique will prevent your team from forming strong bonds of mutual support and cooperation, leading to an isolated and fractured workforce. Think of yourself as a Lioness, separating and scattering the herd before going in for the kill!

Seriously, you must avoid finding out personal details about your team. Don't ask about their family, their dreams or their ambitions, as more than likely they will respond positively to this and unwittingly disclose additional skills and experience that you did not know they possessed. Remember, they are a number, and that is all you need to know. What do you care if their hobby gives them insight into a new product that you are developing, or that their experience in volunteering has given them understanding of dealing with difficult people.

Helpful hints

* Talk lots about yourself, but never ask about your staff.

* If you accidently remember something about someone, pretend you forgot.

* Mix up people's names on a weekly basis – Daily if you sense any positive feelings.

* Never show understanding or compassion when they face difficult situations.

5) Shout at people when things outside of their control happen

How you react to situations and events outside of your control will define you as a manager. Only the weak make allowances for external factors and so you must be strong. Be very strong. In fact, the less influence or control that you or your staff have over something that has happened, the louder your anger must appear. Let it rip as they say! Make sure your staff know that you hold them accountable, even though it can in no way be their fault. You must keep your resolve in this as some foolish members of the team may have the audacity to suggest that it was the fault of some outside influence. Do not let that logical and reasonable argument persuade you. Oh no, everything is in your control, and thus by definition, your team's. Make sure they know it and shout it out so that everyone can hear.

For anyone that works with customers, children or suppliers, then you will have ample opportunity to deploy this most basic of strategies to wind up your staff. The great thing is, that once you start shouting, it may trigger some of your team to start as well. Perfect! A team that shouts together doesn't achieve much else. A key point to remember is that you must never shout at the real cause of the problem, like a misbehaving child, or an obviously incorrect customer. No - you must focus your energy on the team member that had no control – and thus ensure that they will be fuming and unproductive for at least a week.

Helpful hints

* Bring up past mistakes and have another shout about them.

* If someone starts making sense, just shout louder.

* Use the phrase 'you should have done more' when there was absolutely no more anyone could have done.

6) As part of a senior management structure, make sure that you all disagree on important processes and then proceed to give your staff mixed messages

There is nothing more satisfying than seeing your team hopelessly bewildered because you and your senior colleagues disagree on nearly everything. It is a joy to experience the exasperated sighs as yet another process is reviewed and alternately praised, then criticised, then praised etc, leaving your staff wondering who likes what they do and who hates it. Some Bad Managers have perfected this art to such an extent that they themselves criticise improvements and procedures that they have previously introduced. Wonderful stuff! This technique is guaranteed to drive your staff batty.

To enjoy maximum benefit from this strategy, first make sure that you get rid of any consistency from your management style. This is essential, as consistency and cohesion are guaranteed to provide a stable foundation for your team, and that, as we all know, is not what we want! In team meetings, when a senior colleague introduces a new procedure or idea, wait till everyone has absorbed the detail and agreed it is good, then start to disagree. Timing is crucial – make sure that everyone realises that whatever way they decide to do something, they will upset and annoy at least one senior manager.

Helpful hints

* It is a good idea to never settle in an opinion, as it is then easier to keep changing it.

* You can go covert and not disagree publicly, waiting until you get a team member on their own – this enables maximum surprise value.

7) Acknowledge the strength of an employee, then ignore their advice

A quick way to demotivate staff is to ignore their expert advice. Some managers, unfortunately, try to encourage people by actually listening to them when they provide advice, or give research/evidence based ideas. I know – can you believe it! They honestly don't mind some upstart junior colleague being better informed or more creative than themselves. The bad manager, however, will always escape such motivating situations by totally ignoring any such sound advice. It is, of course, much better to flap around in the dark, so to speak.

This technique works best on people that are employed in specialist teams or positions. Additionally, using patronising language when explaining why their thoughts are useless really adds a certain quality of expression to your delivery. Naturally, you will want to introduce your rejections with phrases like, 'When you have more experience...' or 'I've been doing this for a long time, so I know what I am doing...' to emphasise that really it is you who are the expert.

Helpful hints

* Make sure you ask them to back up their ideas with huge quantities of evidence (meaning more work for them), then ignore it anyway.

* In meetings ask the person to the left of the expert what they think. It is fun to watch people in the room exchange glances with the 'expert' with the, 'Why aren't they asking you that question?' expression!

8) Be inconsistent in the way that you deal with people

Treating people equally is a popular thing to do amongst the general manager population, but to be a bad manager one must not follow the crowd. A simple strategy here is to use the daily dice of decision. Write your staff names on some dice and roll them daily, whoever it lands on is a target for the day! Be nice or nasty to them for the day. It's important to have both a positive and negative feature here as it creates the most confusion. Imagine being told all of Monday that you are doing a good job and then on Tuesday you seem to be the most inept and useless worker the boss has ever hired! Guaranteed confusion. After a week or so of this your staff will not know why they are being made to feel nice or worthless.

You should try to avoid any explainable patterns like 'oh the boss is always grumpy on a Tuesday morning and such like. The key here is to be as random and unexpected as possible. Be like the wind; with people never really knowing which way it is going to blow. Even better, can you be like a whirlwind, blowing in different directions during one day? Another good technique to use is that of telling other staff members differing things about someone. When they inevitably talk and share their experiences, they will realise that they are no closer to understanding what you think of them, in fact they may be even more confused.

Helpful hints

* Praise some staff for something and criticise others for exactly the same thing!

* Give pleasant or dismissive answers in team meetings for no apparent reason.

* Never let staff go for more than a few days without a reversal of attitude towards them.

9) Have favourites and give them help to pass appraisals

The very thought of being fair to your staff should send a shiver down your spine, as fairness breeds teamwork, which breeds increased enjoyment and an uplift in the team's abilities, skills and practices. Thus, to avoid this happening, the Bad Manager can employ this tried and tested technique. It will certainly mean that some of your staff spend much of their time being jealous of any others who receive favourable treatment and, more often than not, a healthy amount of resentment and bitterness will develop, culminating in otherwise effective staff leaving. Sounds good right?

You can cause much confusion if you rotate round your staff who you treat favourably. Think of it as a 'flavour of the month' type of thing. Now it is important to realise that you should use every opportunity to praise your 'favourite' whilst dismissing the value of others. This will ensure that the favourite actually resents you as well, meaning that you won't have any staff that genuinely like you. You can even take delight in building someone up to believe they are amazing, only to watch them fail miserably later on.

Helpful hints

* Make sure you don't keep a favourite for too long, or the team will get wise to this technique.

* Interrupt other people's presentations to say how wonderful your favourite is.

* Let the favourite get away with things others are criticised for.

* Give them help to pass appraisals and see the rest of the team burn with anger!

10) Form a negative opinion about someone and then never allow yourself to see past that

Only the truly weak make mistakes so if you have a member of your team who makes one, treat this as proof that they are worthless and never allow any subsequent success to change your view. Honestly, this is a real diamond in the Bad Managers repertoire. Making sure that a team member knows that nothing they can do is good enough is one of the fastest ways to get rid of them. It really is astoundingly successful. Second chances are for wimps. Some might say that mistakes happen for a variety of reasons but we know the truth – they are only made through incompetence!

Initially, you will need to decide who you want to get rid of, and then focus on them for as long as it takes (it won't be long). If you wish to rise to the title of 'Extraordinarily gifted bad manager' you might want to try this technique out on several people at the same time. Everybody loves a double leaving party! The hardest part of using this approach is that you will need to remember that no matter how good any subsequent work, or idea is, you must not show even the slightest hint of gratitude or pleasure.

Helpful hints

* Practise your stony faced expression in the mirror – you don't want them reading your mind

* Try to find fault in everything they do, no matter how small.

* If someone praises them, be quick to bring up something that you don't like to counteract this.

* Ignore evidence of good quality work, regardless of how others present it to you.

11) Interrupt people when they are talking

Simple, yet highly effective. Some might even say that this technique borders on the downright rude, however, it is a fabulous little device designed to maximise irritation and build up annoyance. The more annoyed your staff are, the more likely they will start to look at other opportunities and places to work. It is a strange fact of life that everyone likes to be listened to, and so as a bad manager you must not allow people the feeling that they have had an audience, or that their feelings and thoughts have had time to be adequately expressed.

There are countless opportunities in every working day for you to exercise this idea:

* Waiting for coffee

* Waiting for the toilet

* In a team meeting

* When people are talking to customers

* When you have asked them to talk about something!

As you can see, some situations may cause mere irritation, like a mosquito bite, while others are more akin to having a tiger bite your arm off – it can cause severe frustration!

Helpful hints

* Time your interruptions for maximum impact.

* If they keep talking, just raise your voice even louder.

* Loudly discipline anyone else that interrupts people (you want to demonstrate hypocrisy in action!).

12) Don't listen to staff when they are explaining things for your benefit

Not being listened to is one of the main reasons for dissatisfaction at work. If you can correctly engineer situations where your staff feel that they are not being listened to, then they will stop bothering you in the first place. This has several benefits. Firstly, in team meetings hardly anyone will talk, as they know it is a pointless exercise. Secondly, your team won't come to you with suggestions on how to 'improve' things. Once they realise that you don't want to hear what they have to say, they will content themselves with muttering to other team members.

For a really destructive outcome, be especially careful to ignore wise advice and suggestions that are directed towards safeguarding your team from a legal or regulatory perspective. Opening yourself up to risks that were foreseeable, identifiable and preventable will surely make your team members frustrated. Seeing you decide to remain blissfully ignorant, or wilfully ignorant, is sure to drive them to distraction, (and hopefully out the building!)

Helpful hints

* Pretend that you know better.

* Distract them by taking the conversation off on something completely irrelevant.

* Say, "I'll consider it." Then never think about it again. When they come and ask what you have thought about it, make out like their idea is new. Repeat till they stop coming back!

13) Give staff responsibility and then micro manage what they do

Have you ever wondered how you can quash the enthusiasm of bright, ambitious workers? Well here is a technique for you. Give them some form of responsibility (the bigger the better) and, instead of letting them show what they are capable of, start to micro manage everything they do. I mean, really micro manage everything. Seriously, make sure you get to the point where they feel that they might as well not do anything unless you tell them to first. (Then, the truly Bad Manager can combine this with technique 21) which will leave the hapless worker totally demoralised and demotivated.

There are several different approaches that you can use to achieve your goal here. Give the team member the chance to run a meeting based on their area, and then use other meetings after this to totally change what was agreed or suggested. This approach has the benefit of giving your employee a rollercoaster style journey of emotions, from the "I'm feeling great about my meeting," to the "Wait... what... I thought...," when the realisation hits that nothing they have done has been valued, accepted or implemented! Priceless! An equally effective approach is to say no to every idea they have. Even more frustrating for some is to allow them a budget, but then refuse to sign off on things that they want to spend on, and then use the budget for things you want, but don't tell them that that's what you are going to do!

Helpful hints

* The more you can interfere with your staff, the better.

* Ask other staff to 'support' someone, when they really don't need it – it really bugs them.

* Ask them to prove something works before trying out a new idea – don't give them opportunities to learn and grow through risk taking.

14) Never trust your staff

Just compare the two columns in this list and you will see that clearly, trusting your staff can ONLY lead to disaster! I mean, the other stuff never really happens does it?

What happens if you trust your staff	What happens if you don't trust your staff
Increased sense of employee self worth	Decreased employee self belief
Increased motivation to perform well	Increased apathy
Increased willingness to take risks to achieve the impossible	Decreased creativity
Increased dedication to the job	Increased boredom
Increased personal and corporate loyalty from staff	Decreased loyalty

Helpful hints

* Hover near your staff's area of work to 'watch them' – this will make them nervous which usually leads to them messing up more.

* Constantly check what they have done, adding to their workload. Be inconsistent with the feedback that you give to different people.

* Don't believe anything that they tell you – assume you know better, even though your staff are the only ones who know anything about the relevant situation.

15) Don't find out anything that is important to them

Avoiding a feeling of togetherness and shared purpose within the team you manage is the hallmark of a bad manager. For when people understand their common goal, and each other, great things tend to happen. It is, therefore, crucial that you take all possible steps to create a sense of isolation in each and every person in your team. Make no effort to discover anything other than their name and their basic function within the team. Birthdays are out, names of their significant others and children should be deleted from your memory and all references to hobbies, interests and life outside of work should be rigorously eradicated. Your goal is to get them to feel that you don't know the real them.

A step up from this personal attack, is to encourage the same kind of thing between team members. Making highly visible shows of anger at the disclosure of personal information will lead to a defensive posture from all. Indeed, you want to create and then sustain a climate of fear. Wouldn't it be great if people were scared to share about themselves? Perhaps you could lead some scornful laughter whenever a team member divulges personal preferences? To accomplish this, you will need to lay on the sarcasm, disbelief and attempt to belittle and dismiss even the slightest breath of individualism.

Helpful hints

* Ban personal items form desks/walls and workspaces – you don't want people reminded of the good things in their lives.

* Discourage team building games and social chats – make shared spaces awkward to relax in – perhaps by being in there yourself at key times.

* Make insincere comments about people so that they don't feel comfortable around you..

16) Ask them to choose between you and their family

People are just there to work for you right? I mean, you are the most important person in the world, and no one else should worry about anything other than pleasing you. So when you are dealing with your workers, remember that work should always come before family. Don't let the benefits of a community rich life blind you or entice you to raise the happiness of your staff by letting them go to family events or support and care for people they love! Happy people will ruin your team by infecting others with a sense of satisfaction and contentment that you just don't want.

To make sure your staff are properly demotivated, make sure they know that there is no point asking for time away, or even to work flexibly, to attend things like weddings/funerals/class assemblies and the like. Also, if their dependents are ill, then make life as difficult as possible for them. I mean sick kids can take care of themselves can't they! Surely every parent is more than happy to leave their disgusting offspring with others when they are unwell. Honestly, it's just selfish of people to want to care for others!

Helpful hints

* Never admit that other human beings are important.

* Refuse to accept that sometimes people come before work.

* Keep reminding people of how they have let you down by putting family situations first.

* Model being horrible to your own family (if you have one) so others can see the right way of treating people.

17) Make sure your staff never know if now is the 'right time' to ask you a question

Quite often, you as a manger will be approached by your staff asking for advice or to seek an opinion on a suggested improvement they have come up with. This presents you with a delicious opportunity to make them squirm and hover outside your door, trying to guess if you will a) bite their head off b) laugh at their inexperience or c) take you seriously. This is an opportunity for your staff to realise that they are playing Russian roulette! Using this technique will immediately put them into a nervous state, cloud their thinking and allow you to dominate the brief meeting. After all, they are just interrupting you and should be off somewhere working right?

The key here is to make sure that you are so inconsistent that no one has a clue what mood you will be in at any given time. For example, start the day with a cheery hello, but then immediately launch into full on attack mode when someone asks you a question. If you can record these encounters you will enjoy watching their shocked expressions when you play it back to yourself. Make sure that you don't get into a routine, variety is essential and so this technique requires dedication and practise.

Helpful hints

* Have some decision dice with labels like 1- Annoying 2- Dragon 3- Nice etc

* Keep a record (like a bingo chart) and try and bewilder as many people in one day as you can – don't forget, you can be nice to them sometimes as it just encourages them to come back another time when you can use other techniques mentioned here to lay into them!

* Install a secret camera outside your door so you can watch people nervously pacing, wondering if they should knock on your door.

* In team meetings inform staff that you have an 'open door policy' (just don't tell them that it's dangerous to come through that door!

18) Tell them you want something done a certain way, then shout at them that it is wrong when they do it that way

Nothing causes more irritation, annoyance and despair in your staff then this technique. It is a shining example of how to not only bring hardworking members of your team to tears, but ensure that they go into full meltdown mode. When contemplating using this technique, you should check that the morale level is already low, as this won't work against a team that is highly motivated and has a good team atmosphere (they will just group together against you). Instead, you must choose this strategy carefully, when the herd is scattered so to speak, and you have identified an animal on its own!

This strategy works well in conjunction with no 3, as you will add to their sense of confusion and helplessness. They truly won't know what to do, and believe that nothing they do is good enough. Keeping people guessing what they should do, and destroying their confidence is a sure fire way of getting them out the door! When people realise that even when they do what you say, they will still be wrong, then they will start heading for the exits.

Helpful hints

* Be sneaky and get some deputies to announce new policies (that you agreed) and then go out and cause mayhem by attacking the policies.

* Don't keep any formal record of changes or decisions so that you can argue that it is other people who remember things wrong.

* Confuse staff by complimenting one person and criticising another when they have both completed it as you requested.

19) Tell them not to eat anything with sugar in

Someone made you the boss. So, act like it everywhere and anywhere you can. Make sure that your staff know that you have power over them in every aspect of their lives (at least, that's what you want them to feel). When staff do nice things for each other (a common example being cakes for birthdays) make sure that you loudly and continuously disprove and try to make people feel as guilty as possible for enjoying them. After all, no one else is able to make decisions that are right, so you must do it for them. How dare they believe that they have choices in life. They must do things your way, which definitely means no sugar at work!

You can extend this type of attitude towards staff parties and social get togethers. Essentially, you want to be known as a killjoy. If, when you walk into the room, conversation stops and people make excuses to leave, then you are getting it right. Now the great part is this; when everyone else has left the room, you can stuff yourself full of all the left over cakes! It's perfect.

Helpful hints

* When conversation seems to be heading towards a pleasant subject, start expressing disapproval.

* Constantly remind people of the evil of their choices.

* Give names to areas where people stack cakes like 'the corner of early death' to terrify your staff.

20) Don't ask them for ideas

Your staff are useless and lack imagination; they don't have anything new to offer and any idea that they would likely give is worthless. In fact, you run the risk of becoming like them if you allow yourself to listen to their ill-thought out and dangerous notions of improvement. Be on your guard at all times. Actually - let's face it - the best strategy is to take cover in your office and try to ignore your staff as much as possible. Whatever you do, don't ask them for ideas, as you are bound to raise their motivation level as they will think that you want to hear what they have to say!

If you have set the correct general atmosphere then this final technique should prove no obstacle to you. It will allow you to wallow in your current situation with no fear of improvement coming your way. You will continue to relish the feelings of uncertainty and anxiety about your job, as your team will be ineffective and disjointed. Perfect.

Helpful hints

* Have stock responses like 'it's ok, your ideas are useless' ready to respond to unwanted suggestions.

* Make sure that any staff that have developed further qualifications are ruthlessly ignored so that not even the smallest piece of relevant, up to date advice makes its way into your team.

33788656R00025

Printed in Great Britain
by Amazon